AF505308

Wolf's Clothing

Photo © by Peter Moore, 1974.

Wolf's Clothing

Rillo

Left Hand Books

The publisher wishes to thank the John W. and Clara C. Higgins Foundation and the Pauline Oliveros Foundation for financial assistance granted.

Cover painting is by Bryan McHugh and based on an image of a coyote-like animal appearing on a bowl made by a Mimbres Indian potter.

Designed by Bryan McHugh.

ISBN 1-880516-12-8

Manufactured in the United States of America.

for
Walter Bianco

Introduction
by
Susan Smith Nash

Coyote breaks the law and gets away with it. But, instead of frustrating, the transgressions delight. Do we want so badly to defeat the law? If we could defeat the law, could we defeat what the law is all about? Law is death. It's always been like that—and Rillo realizes it. So, enter Coyote, or any one of Coyote's doubles—Cody Jarrett, Hermes, the gang, they're all in *Wolf's Clothing,* a celebration of transformation, metamorphosis, and breaking the law of death.

Rillo's coyote is a heartbreaker, an outlaw, a gangster *and* his moll, a wild-at-the-teeth furred purveyor of the unconscious who never gets caught nosing up the latch on the henhouse or rifling the till. So, not surprisingly, Rillo's *Wolf's Clothing* is pure play—it teases the reader with phase changes and costuming, and it parades forth the full spectrum of multiplicities of identity. Yet, paradoxically, given the protean nature of the work, *Wolf's Clothing* is a highly structured work, and the stanzas possess a regular arrangement of end-rhyme and iambic feet. In the tension between formal structure and free verse, Rillo explores how transformations occur at the margins—not the margins of language, but the margins of the law. Rillo constructs a poetic nether region which exists along the boundary between a law-

i

abiding, rule-following prosodic structure, and an untamed heart of darkness in which all the beasts of the unconscious reside.

By leading the reader into this decentering, defamiliarizing boundary region, Rillo teaches the reader how to raid our culture and our collective unconscious in order to develop procedures for understanding how identity can be formed and then reformed. Going into such a boundary region can apply to notions of one's own sense of identity. "Plunder the till," says Coyote. This is the first step on the way to freedom which accompanies self-transformation. It also signals a rupturing, where all the cultural beliefs, values, symbols, etc. rise to the surface. In Coyote's world, one must transgress in order to metamorphose, in order to be alive.

Coyote is the primary player in *Wolf's Clothing*. The other characters quickly reveal themselves to be variations, however complex, of Coyote. Coyote & Co. are tricksters extraordinaire. They "take free verse...work it like a spell" on the reader, and on language itself. Rillo's use of syntax is subtly subversive—it seems to be straightforward enough, but its quick convolutions and subject shifts reveal that it is a highly innovative form in deceptive clothing. Because it is a more seamless, melodious form than

Dada or collage, *Wolf's Clothing* may seem to contain one voice, and yet, the work is a complex inter-related, resonating, polyphonous composition.

Yet, despite the polyphony, Coyote's voice predominates. As a trickster figure, Coyote evokes what Erich Neumann has characterized as the transformation myth: "Nature rules over nature." Coyote's wiliness makes this species more effective than humans to rule nature, and to position itself at the top of the power hierarchy, even on the same level as the gods, especially Hermes. With the ability to change form, Coyote and the deities can dominate, control, order (or disorder) external reality. Coyote dramatizes the moment of art production, and what results is a theater which elaborates how transformations of reality occur. What Coyote allows is insight or intellection of how one might undergo the process of self-reification.

In *The Origins and History of Consciousness,* Erich Neumann suggests that this knowledge is gained at the point of maximum confrontation with one's own mortality. As one becomes aware of death, the life-death contrast is at its most extreme:

when the personality experiences dying as a simul-
taneous act of self-reproduction, will two-fold self
be reborn as the total self. Accordingly, in the Ti-
betan Book of the Dead, the dead and the dying are
summoned to a visionary knowledge of this repro-
ductive act. ...[it is] a form of self-generation.
(Neumann 2550).

In *Wolf's Clothing,* Rillo veils the presence of death, but only
slightly. Death is there, but it is cloaked and robed in Machine
Gun Kelly pinstripe woven of polyphonic voices which simulta-
neously talk like characters on the lam in an old black and white
gangster movie, Old West outlaws rowdying up a saloon, and
Hermes up to his old games. The desert creates the perfect back-
drop for Rillo's playful voicings. The characters cavort upon a
technicolor screen that transforms itself in wash after wash of
supersaturated tones. The desert performs elaborate veilings,
"laying down track over track" to outwit the law.

Yet, sooner or later, Rillo sorts and separates each set of tracks
so we can hear the individual voices. If the voices seem strangely
prophetic, even apocalyptic, it's no accident. Apocalypse involves

an unveiling and a glimpse into the *sanctum sanctorum*. At points, Rillo lifts the veil and we see Coyote's rites and procedures—the knowledge of death is what we become aware of. What death signifies is a private and personal apocalypse that sets self-generating processes into motion.

> Coyote goes out with a bang
> *and* a whimper "Made it ma!
> Top of the world." He sets the lan-
> guage, then himself on fire. Apo-
> calypse bow-wow. Top? More like
> end of the world.

Coyote sets himself on fire. This brings to mind a horrific vision—shades of the Vietnam War and the indelible image of orange-robed Buddhist monks immolating themselves to protest the violence, the senseless killings of entire villages. Rillo's work possesses a complex depth with its sometimes unsettling vision of the unconscious. Perhaps the vibrancy of Rillo's work hinges upon a willingness to ironize Coyote's personal, artistic apocalypse, instead of sentimentalizing the situation or turning it into melodrama. In fact, in the world of the coyote, apocalypse is at the root of every act of life and art and self-expression. It is a linguistic apocalypse and Rillo's "language on fire" echoes Jacques Derrida's notions that apocalypse can occur at the language level, and that it has to do with the fact that meaning tends to melt down just when you think you've got it pinned down.

Rillo suggests that language is remarkably resistant to entrapment, and thus Coyote wriggles free of the rigid grammars which might keep its paw in a painful trap. In *Wolf's Clothing*, Coyote is free, and his words freely move in and out of the words of others—of Cody Jarrett, of his gang, of Hermes. Communication is not a matter of confining signification to a cage. What occurs has been described by Jacques Derrida in *Grammatology* and *Signesponge*. Alan Thiher articulates Derrida's position:

> In a world in which the divine guarantees of logos have disappeared and essentialist thought has lost its power to convince, Derrida proposes conceptual play as a substitute for theologically underwritten meaning (Thiher 89).

Rillo suggests there is no essentialist nature, no prime essence, things do not have a single, essential, basic nature, and there is no ontological certainty. All identity results of a sleight-of-mind. The essentialist nature rests squarely in the possibility that all is illusion. The trickster makes shape out of maya (illusion). So, Coyote is not so much shape-*shifter* as shape-*maker*.

Rillo connects Coyote, Cody Jarrett, Hermes, and the gang by a thread, or even "strings made of sheep-gut." Yet, they serve a dual function—the threads not only make connections, they also can be played in order to make music, or make art. Hermes plays the strings for all they're worth. What Rillo suggests is that for Hermes, and for all transformations, the strings make the instrument. Once Hermes (or Rillo) strings the lyre, the music will sound. The instrument will not be playable until it has strings. In a like manner, identity is not recognizable until it has threads, or connections to other identities.

The process of making connections, threading or stringing identities together, parallels the myth of Ariadne, whose threads allowed one to escape the minotaur's labyrinth. In *Ariadne's Thread*, J. Hillis Miller points out that the figure of Ariadne's thread provides a model for interpersonal relations which can be extended to imply or suggest sexual (and thereby generative) liaisons. What is going on is the work of self and meaning construction. The process is *anastomosis,* which Miller defines:

> *Anastomosis:* image of a line joining two vessels or enclosures, in this case from person to person, like a telephone line (Miller 144).

Yet, when Ariadne weaves her thread, and a spider spins its web, the image of a line connecting two points is expanded so that linearity takes on all the intricacy of an enormous web. There are interlinking circular, concentric workings out. The connections are often tangential, and they bear geometrical relations to each other, rather than sharing an intersection point.

For Rillo, metamorphosis and apocalypse conjoin as Coyote, Cody Jarrett, Hermes, and the other characters reflect upon each other, their textural presences interweaving in endlessly criss-crossing concentric circles. The function of the web is multiple, and the process of anastomosis is complex: they create webs of self, and yet the culturally-held conception of the created self (Coyote, a gangster, Hermes, etc.) may crawl along the web, spiderlike, and entomb and devour the text-generated self. This may express the tensions that always exist between the culture at large and the constructed world of the text—the meanings that emerge are always in flux, and always under negotiation.

Imagine: Coyote with *The Kiss of the Spider Woman*—it's a trickster tale through a convex mirror. "Coyote plays his whistle / and the sky turns red." The landscape of *Wolf's Clothing* is a gorgeously surreal mixture of the film and the filmed, the natural and the artificed, the ordered and the disordered. Shifts of identity occur within the poem to the point that survival is problematized in the constant negotiations occuring between reader and the text—at times "a wolf pack / now occupies the public's mind." There are great surprises unveiled by the force of the trickster's spell. Coyote pulls the wraps off identity, and the Coyote's voice of the wilderness is an insistent yapping, howling, moaning over what it cannot stop craving—fresh eggs, rodents, trash, all the human detritus that promises explanations about the strange ways we live our lives. Coyote catches us chewing our fleas, attempting to reconcile ourselves with the cultural forces that threaten to engulf us.

Wolf's Clothing reinforces the idea that humans are not invincible, and that the individual reader is vulnerable to Coyote's insistent intrusions into humankind's tendency toward hubris. Coyote is not stopped, even by our best defenses—Coyote continues, tracking up our unconscious, disordering our structures against fear, as he makes his way tipping over trash cans, unlatching the gates that threaten to barricade us from our own human spirits. Coyote opens the door for us. He, like our own language, is full of surprises. Language is always poised, like Coyote, to yank the blanket from the bed.

Susan Smith Nash
April 3, 1994

Works Cited

Miller, J. Hillis. *Ariadne's Thread: Story Lines*. New Haven: Yale UP, 1992.
Neumann, Erich. *The Origins and History of Consciousness*. Transl. R. F. C. Hull. Foreword by C. G. Jung. Princeton: Princeton UP, 1954.
Thiher, Alan. *Words in Reflection: Modern Language Theory and Postmodern Fiction*. Chicago: U of Chicago P, 1984.

Wolf's Clothing

I begun to think how dreadful it was, even for murderers, to be in such a fix. I says to myself, there ain't no telling but I might come to be a murderer myself yet, and then how would I like it?

Coyote and desert hare
caption and shibboleth
one's hard to scare
the other's scared to death.

The hare takes the vertical
while you get the bed.
Coyote plays his whistle
and the sky turns red.

Never fear. Now what do you lack?
Here: the coyote's minus sign
the desert hare's awesome black
lyre: time's nick and its anodyne.

Coyote's holed up again
it's come down to the wire.
On the shelf next to a can
of ecocide the hare's lyre.

Semaphor. Danger. Coyote.
Double trouble and savoir faire.
Trickster and ally to three
pieces in the form of a hare.

A hideout. At wit's end a dream
Kidnapping a volcano
You in or out? A hare-brained scheme
how can the coyote say no!

Coyote wolfs down ten bowls
of sugar-coated violence;
milk running out his bullet holes.
This kid survives by his sixth sense.

Coyote forgets his one line.
He walks out of the film noir
and swipes the infrared kine
the ephebe is now an outlaw.

Wanted: coyote, hardcore
villain at large; his face
hid by a mask—shy predator
description without a trace.

Is it a coyote
we're after or a where
wolf; a beast in peyote
vision, or wary stranger?

That's a coyote not a wolf.
And that's a lyre not a zither.
No strings attached: silent, aloof.
I'll play it if you slither hither.

Trickster beyond good and evil.
A bank robber. His paws hover
then plunge in and rifle the till.
"He went that way." For cover

the hare's smoke and mirrors. One last
long take. A jig-sawed coyote
in leg irons; sky stretched past
its limit of opacity.

The string breaks, released from the hand's
blistring art; an atavistic poise
replaces its grip. Love, sweet love brands
the lyre, now free to sing of boys.

The hare pulls a fast one.
"My crafty lyre for your inchoate
chant." Coyote howls at the sun.
The shy transgressor now a poet.

Night falls on our band of reivers:
the hare and coyote; their fell
accomplice, the lyre, takes free verse
literally, works it like a spell.

Coyote dreams of his cohort
an aspiring cat burglar, infernal
sweetie-pie. They're wed at the court-
house. Handcuffs bind the criminal

groom to his wily bride. Above
the law one day, brought down by it
the next—imprisoned by love.
At least neither has started to cry, yet.

The lyre receives an uneven share
of the loot. Hey, he's just been strung
along. "What if he sings," the hare
warns. "No chance, the cat's got his tongue

and he's too perplexed, he can't think
of anything to say, a scare-
dy cat with a killer's instinct,"
says the coyote to the hare.

Coyote plans a new caper.
He quickly assembles his gang,
all but the lyre who's in stir.
A patois of criminal slang

and loony tunes will combine
and overwrite his primal speech.
A new vernacular will shine
in place of baby talk. Jail will teach

this lyre a lesson. After ten
years he'll emerge; a smooth
talker. Who'd guess this broken
toy would still have the power to sooth

the likes of the outlaw Cody
Jarrett and his gang. Not so fast
It's not Cody, but Coyote
he's the mad dog heading this cast.

Coyote's now prey to doubt.
A wolf eclipses him as public
enemy; media hype out-
strips the lyre's panegyric.

Bad luck now dogs the princely whelp
and his bandit crew. Coyote's hurt
in a stick-up; his pals will help
count the loot, what else. The desert

won't give up its refugee.
It lays down track over track
to put the law off track. Coyote
escapes capture, even death. Implac-

able no man's land will take care
of its wounded animal. Canyons,
mountain lion caves hide the Jar-
rett gang; coyote's companions

fan out in search of more loot
while he licks his wounds. Coyote's
a marked man, so are they. It's shoot
or be shot. At least aim to please.

Cut to the criminal's hideout.
The wily Hermes appears
with his trusty lyre. Sharp-eyed scout,
bandit, and still in diapers.

Here we have an unwanted child
and a wanted man wrapped in one.
Coyote snatches up both—mild
transgressor and his invention.

He can't live on bread and water.
The wily rascal's not yet weaned
from nectar. Wanted for manslaughter!
This divine tot, a suckling your fiend!

Coyote writes at white heat
"The Cattle Rustler, a Noh
play," on back of his rap sheet
The four-legged bandit's exploits show

through the archaic text. The scrap
proof coyote's led a double
life. Neither pose really does cap-
ture him: bard, thief, both mean trouble.

The cops devise a legal snare.
Coyote's caught red-handed. Sing-
Sing next stop. Railroaded. The hare
switches the train to a siding.

Coyote needs an alibi.
A ready-made lyre, its red-
handed minstrel. A lullabye,
Quick, let's put the law to bed.

Coyote goes out with a bang
and a whimper. "Made it ma!
Top of the world." He sets the lan-
guage, then himself on fire. Apo-

calypse bow-wow. Top? More like end
of the world "But my wolf's clothing
is fire-proof." Flamous last words. Incen-
diary speech. The fear and loathing

he inspires makes him more dan-
gerous than ever. No one dare
touch his frowning form. Mark of Cain-
nine preserves this holy terror.

Coyote leaves the hare for dead.
But at the last second goes back
for the lyre, and he too gets fed
to the wolves—as a bedtime snack.

Coyote, cat and hare: a black
lyre costs each his life. Legend
translates and obscures; a wolf pack
now occupies the public's mind.

Coyote sings praise to the lord
of hip-hop; the hare to Egypt's
Thoth. Magic lyre smashed; its cord
used to string up the culprits.

The desert travels with relics
of the holy blissful varmint
a pay-per-view X-ray depicts
him in a convict's striped garment.

I felt a little heavy-hearted about the gang,
but not much, for I reckoned if they could stand it,
I could.

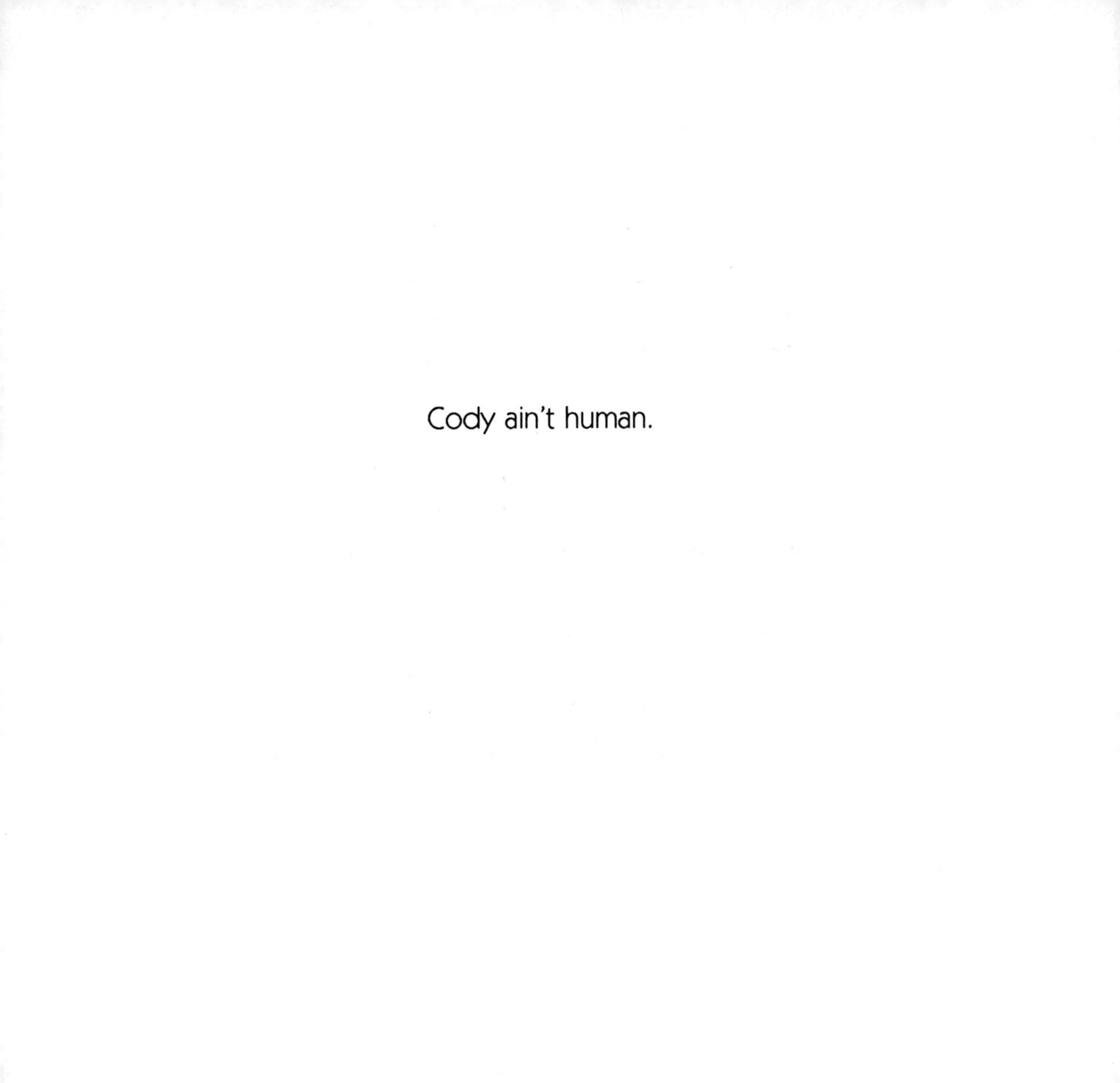

Cody ain't human.

"There's insanity in the Jarrett family."
The headaches he faked as a boy
foreshadowed the actual pain
splitting our train-robber the coy-

ote in two, leaving each half
to wail in dire woe. Meanwhile, far
from coyote's hideout in the Cal-
ifornia Sierra, his avatar

watches loony tunes. The images
of the hare and the coyote flicker
in the gloomy, thick-shaded cave.
As bold and cunning as they come, quicker

than death, Hermes can match the outlaw
for wiles. Jarrett's cartoon counterpart's
high-tech plans backfire. The coyote
sends away for a kit and he starts

from the blueprint included with
Acme's ready-to-assemble kits.
"If that battery's dead,
it'll have company." Jarrett's

Headaches recur, each attack
more violent than the last.
"And now back to the adventures
of coyote." Hermes must act fast

or he'll miss the next episode.
What's more, the danger a noonday prowler
risks in being seen isn't lost on him.
One day old, already past the crawler

stage and who should the spry rascal meet
at the threshold of the high-roofed cave?
Why a creature—an amphibian—tramping
on all fours. "Friend, you're in peril! But I'll save

you from danger." The tortoise, finding
itself at an awkward crossroads,
stops, too self-effacing to go around
the god. A stick of dynamite explodes

in the coyote's face. "Cody is it?
You've got a good memory for names,
too good." "I fear you'll come to grief
if you linger here. These woods host games

of cops and robbers. If you still insist
on hoofing it through these woods, I won't stop
you." A plank holds the rock in place. Right
when the time comes to roll it off the top

of the cliff the boulder slides backwards and
flattens the coyote. Some new endeavor
will bring him back to life. So let's shift
from the scene of our cliff-dweller's misfor-

tune back to the adventures of Hermes.
"Open up and you won't get hurt."
"And the way faring Traveller
For ever open is his door." The pert

little lad wants the turtle for a toy.
Outright intimidation fails
nine times in ten. Besides "lots of people
have guns." Not this wily god, he assails

the turtle by taunting it... with both hands
he raised it up.... "You're not going anywhere
Jarrett. Put your hands up where I can see them."
Running back into his abode, the car-

apace tucked beneath his arm, Hermes set
to making the lyre. He worked at white heat.
He cut stalks, pulling the measured reeds through
holes punctured in the shell's rim. For his next feat

he stretched oxhide round the shell. He took strings
made of sheep-gut, the wires held by a crosspiece
fixed to two branches, handsomely curved
but solid arms. The god worked with increas-

ing speed and the lyre was soon finished.
"A week has passed since bandits jumped a mail train
coming out of the high sierra tunnel..."
The road snakes its way up the mountain

This time the badlands hidalgo
and mesa-top trickster will succeed
in bagging his lightning-fast prey.
The mountain wall, rising straight up, will impede

the racing bird. A road sign. Its arrow points
left. Look again. Some cunning sprite or fer-
al child has contrived a detour. Cody
checks his watch, having timed the train robber-

y down to the second. Unlike the
ordinary dog our cartoon canine
possesses an acute sense of per-
spective. The coyote altered the sign

bearing the arrow. The mischievous pup
now rolls on the paint, his tromp l'oeil fresco
of a tunnel poured straight from the can.
One thinks of the cave paintings at Lascaux

as another instance when a picture
was applied to the hunt. "Ed, Cotton,
when we get this train on the spur
start hopping. Go." Coyote waits. The hot sun

burning in the sky, weakens his resolve.
But the predator's craving for his sweet-
tasting prey proves stronger. A streak of white light
zips through the tromp l'oeil tunnel. The coyote

steps in front of the two-dimensional
opening. At that second the mail train
comes out of the tunnel. Cody leaps down
on to it. And the wily, little thane

of Kyllene and Arcadia scampers out
of his cave holding up the gleaming tortoise-
shell toy. "What is this, a hold up"? "We're just
changing engineers." A howling chorus

provides the desert music. The wayward
babe lay in his cradle, looking like the black
night; the sweet lyre at his side even
blacker. While the detectives try to crack

the case, Hermes plays with the covers.
Coyote's desert hymns fill his ears, their spine-
tingling tones soothing the child. Certain no one
can tie him to the theft of the kine

or the tunnel job the boy snuggles into
his sweet-scented blankets, an innocent ba-
by. "Authorities now believe that the gang
has escaped to Arizona where today

a bank was robbed and two tellers killed
with the same cold-bloodedness that charac-
terized the tunnel-robbery. The god's
mother, however, noticed her son slip back

into the cave. The wind roars and shakes the
trees, whirling in shrill eddies around the moun-
tain hideout... The cattle bandit rushes
through the key hole. "Now straight for bed," the scoun-

drel snatching up his lyre as he hops in
"Coyotes are creatures of slinking
and stealthy ways." "Why don't you give them my address."
Coyote Jarrett has to do the thinking

for the gang. "Where do we go after the
second feature"? "You're not going anywhere.
I am. Gonna give myself up."
"I'm on to your tricks, you rascally reiver,

prairie-wolf and all-round varmint. You're up to
mischief. Why, none but burglars and other looting
riff-raff prowl on tip-toes in the dead of night.
A tiny infant and soon you'll be shooting

it out with the cops." The mother chides her
errant son. "Talk plain son." "While those
hoodlums were killing those innocent people on
the train, I was lifting fifty head from Apollo's

herd. Couldn't be in two places at once
could I?" "You're the smartest there is, Coyote"!
"I'm but a baby, how could I carry off
his cattle, being so easily cowed," the doughty

son of Zeus and Maia replied to his
mother's scolding. "I thought I saw a child,
I can't be sure," the informant began.
"I hope I'm not leading you on a wild

goose chase." "These geese we're looking for are
pretty wild." "He followed the horned cows, his switch
cracking over the shambling kine.
That tiny cowherd's whip seemed to bewitch

the herd; they were all switched around, tails
backwards and heads facing toward him.
As the sun was just then setting
I did a double-take." "This shows crim-

inal intent: Reversing the hoofprints."
They're on to our little cowherd. The ruse he
devised to avoid capture, driving the cows
on a beguiling route, didn't work. "Cody

calls charging roadblocks unscientific."
A fast-approaching snowstorm finds the Jarrett
gang on the move. Cody Coyote
gives the orders: "Ed, we'll separate.

Go east until you hit the highway
then double back over the bridge
and stay on dirt roads all the way, you hear."
And the bandits bid adios to their refrig-

erated hideout. "The cottage fades
before his sight." "Who's going to see
a little bit of smoke a hundred miles from
nowhere"? ...and up went the heated smoke. Cody

Jarrett will perish by fire. A fitting end
to this outlaw. For the folk hero tricks-
ter Hermes was the very first fire-
starter. He gave us fire from fire-sticks

and the gentle hymnster's lyre. "Hermes. Never
herd of him," says the nimble cattle thief.
The bandit decides to set aside a few head
from the stolen herd. One hecatomb of beef

when stretched will yield twelve equal portions.
"Are you in for any of it"? "Full share."
"Anything we get coyote's in for
his full share." Moved by his sense of solidar-

ity with the gods Hermes plans to make
a sumptuous meal for them, a real spread.
"Tommy, rustle up some grub." Jarrett
settles for take-out. To barbecue the sacred

meat, the cheerful Hermes breaks the law.
That law forbids children to play with matches.
The wily bandit crouches, his cupped palms
shielding the sparks. The fire quickly catches.

Smoke drifts up through the mesh in the pile of twigs.
"That place is a stack of dynamite"!
He fanned the fire, tossing more kindling on
the heap until the flame rose to a great height.

While the lame Hephaestos, god of accelerants
and the red hot blasting furnace, kin-
dled the fire he went into the barn
and dragged out two prize curved-horned cows, their size no hin-

drance to the super-human herder
of the kine. The wight fell to his task,
dispatching the cows. He hacked the meat, placing
the fatted strips on skewers. His bandit's mask

fitted over mouth and nose. The feral god
sniffed the smoke rising from the fire. He let
the mask slip, hungering for the sacred meat.
Sorely tempted to stuff his holy gullet

yet he resisted the atavistic
craving. This child was far too young to dine
on the succulent roasts and the chops, wrapped
in fat. He lacked a full set of canine

teeth, the choppers needed to chew the meat.
This kid had not yet even begun
to teethe. "Sure you won't try some of this delicious
soup?" He twice refused, now he wants to eat the soup. "Hun-

ger's always a hopeful sign." "Nobody feeds
Coyote Jarrett. What am I a kid"?
"Jarrett's a raving maniac,
they've got him in a straitjacket." That gun hid

up his sleeve will change that. Apollo steps down
the stone threshold and into the gloomy cave
and makes straight for the cradle. Seeing the god
angered over the loss of his cows, the knave

sank down far within his covers and curling
up, head, hands and feet, lay fast asleep.
In fact, he was awake all along;
the child's tortoise-shell tucked, for safe keep-

ing, under his arm. Taking a shining key,
Apollo opened the doors to the cab-
inets lining the cave. In one—"The count-
less gold of the akeing heart." The robber jab-

bered away, knowing but a few words
of baby talk. While his brother made a com-
plete search, checking every niche and nook, the coy
outlaw lay in his cradle, sucking his thumb.

"And these are the gems of the Human Soul
The rubies and pearls of a lovesick eye"
and these the three hundred thousand dollars in
federal currency, the train robber Coy-

ote Jarrett's take from the tunnel job. "O child
lying in the cradle. Out with it! I want
my cows back. Tell me where they are and be quick
about it or I'll swear out a warrant

it was you who made off with them.
No trying to deny it. I can ferret
out cattle-rustling varmints, blindfolded."
"I've just finished my report on Jarrett.

Violent, homicidal and well-versed in
the reiver's art, he'll probably have recur-
rent periods of normal behavior but end up
kicking and screaming in a nut house; a seeker

after the kine, Coyote Jarrett poses
a great danger to both the infrared
herds in the sun and the beasts shuffling
on the terrestrial plane." "I thought you said

cleanest in the west? That mirror's so dirty
you can see double." "How would you like
a little change of scenery, Cody?"
The countryside wraps around a strik-

ing red-figured bowl: "some place where we might
be able to cure your headaches." The young
cattle rustler looks out on the herds. Safe
behind bars, the jailbird can't wait to get sprung.

First chance he gets he springs on the herd.
"You wouldn't mind a little trip?"
It's the god's exploits figured on the bowl.
A hymn mimed in infrared paint. The strip

shows fresh scenes between its borders. Nor will turn-
ing the bowl three sixty degrees bring
the god's adventures full circle. Its designs
cheat the round. The human breath has made this ring

of pictures around the bowl. The masked robber
waits for night. Pursuing his bold plan, the bandit
cuts off from the herd fifty head of loud-
lowing cattle, warning: "Now you know how jit-

tery I am—any minute I'm likely
to explode, now get!" "I turned my back on them
for a split second." That's when the varmint
made his move, leaving him with only a rem-

nant of the original herd. The bowl de-
picts the missing herd in a wavering red
outline. Hermes too. The cattle thief's whip
alone retains its jittery shape. A kindred

trait signals a shared identity: Hermes,
the coyote—his four-legged double.
"Fence fifty get twenty." The keen business
sense gives them away. Why the divine trouble-

maker and the fell train robber are one
and the same. "You bought a gas truck?
What's the matter, forget how to steal one?"
You can't keep Coyote Jarrett down—he's indestruc-

tible! The prison bosses assign Cody
to a work detail. The racket filling
the machine shop mingles with his inner
voices until Jarrett collapses, spilling

several kegs of nails lined up on a shelf.
Down come crashing the hundred pounds of Ac-
me's industrial tacks. Someone has it in
for Coyote Jarrett. "If I turned my back

long enough for you to put a knife in it
there'd be a knife in it." His wife com-
plains, "what's the use of having money if
you got to start running every time some-

body sees a shadow." "What's suspition
in one man is caution in another & truth
or discernment in another & in some
it is folly." Thus writes the poet Blake. The ruth-

less bandit isn't taking any chances.
"Just a feeling I had Cody. I
could've been wrong." "Your hunches are never wrong ma."
"Always on the run, always on the move, the coy-

ote ranges from Canada in the north
to Guatamala in the south, chief-
ly frequenting the open plains on both sides
of the chain of the Rocky Mountains." A brief

visionary trance presages his splitting
headaches. "The stars sun moon all shrink away."
"Don't let them see you like this, might give some of
them ideas." His fit now past, the cattle-slay-

er wakes up to find himself inside
someone else's skin. "I like your tailor
how do you like mine?" "When the tenth moon was fast
set in the sky, a new-born saw the light. A paler

colored, smaller version of the trickster,
this child's more typical of the coyo-
te of the deserts of eastern California,
Nevada and Utah than the one from Io-

wah! The sun's tenant cowherd sees the tortoise shell
and takes it from the child as forfeiture
against his kidnapped kine. The fine satisfies
the aggrieved solar flare but leaves the bandit fur-

ious. The world renowned cattle rustler
and irrepressible trickster has a fierce,
psychopathic devotion to his lyre. Robbed
of the hollow toy, Hermes let out a pierc-

ing scream, swearing he is not the culprit.
"Nor have I seen any one else make off with
your cows. Thieves. Cows. I don't know what these are.
I hear only rumors, vague reports based in myth."

"No clue to their movements has been reported
since their assault on a service station
north of Gallup, New Mexico." Apollo
laughs, predicting: "You'll soon be boring your way in-

to many a secure home, quietly packing
up its contents, and leaving nothing except
the sleeping occupants who'll wake to find they've
been stripped of all their belongings. Some low adept

at reiving has struck," they'll cry, raising the alarm.
"Why, the masked varmint slipped right past the hundred-
eyed dog guarding the house, even swiping its
milk bone biscuit." "It is now assumed by fed-

eral law enforcement agencies
that Jarrett and the other escaped convicts
are heading for California." The beguiling
whelp flatly denied the charges. "The law inflicts

terrible penalties on cattle rustlers,
ruthless train robbers and others of their ilk, met-
ing out to them fines and jail terms." "The man you want,"
Hermes replied, "bears no likeness to me. A repeat

offender, a stalwart felon, unfazed
by the barbed ring put up to protect the herd
against his costly raids—he's your culprit,
not I; a tender babe who hasn't murdered

a single soul or yet received his lumps."
"...this concludes the nightly news summary from
KFKL San Bernadino...and now back
to coyote and roadrunner." "Do you come

peaceable or do I handcuff you?"
"I wish every last cow would perish!"
Placed under arrest for cattle stealing, the child
was fit to be tied. He did, in truth, cherish

the kine: "Wanted: Crane Operator. Ex-
perienced only. The Acme Dem-
olition Firm. Corner of Main and Atlantic
in Alhambra." "A black belt in mayhem!

Look at this resume! Mechanical Genius.
Expert trouble-shooter. I say we hire this Wil
E. Coyote. He's perfect for us." "It ain't like
waiting for some human being who wants to kill

you. Coyote ain't human." "Does that say deft or daft
handler of dynamite?" "I said I'd be back." Death
Valley's unflappable hidalgo and
cagey canine trickster plans to lure his feath-

ered nemesis with a free sample of Acme
bird seed. Using a cynical marketing ploy,
Acme Feed Supply throws in a free stick
of dynamite with each fifty pound bag. Coy-

ote takes from his coat an extra-long fuse.
"Hey, Heck, you're a pretty good man with a blow torch—
suppose you could cut a hole in here and through it
into the tank?" "Seems we're in for another scorcher

and nothing left to eat or drink," the tena-
cious trickster exclaims, shedding his fire-proof hidal-
go's coat. "Dry as a bone"! The wayward fuse circles
a cactus and a pile of stones; its final

loop encloses a lone cow skull, making a kind
of lariat, a crazy temenos
around it. "Into the wooden horse boys."
Even now, held in the law's clutches, the heinous

outlaw tries to wriggle out of the charges.
He denies any connection to the theft
of the cattle; and putting down in writing his side
of the story, the wily deponent signs his deft-

ly-worded deposition.

9C. Running Track of Coyote in Mud. Natural size: FF 1¾" x 2½" HF 1½" x 2¼", 18" leaps.

Sources

Mark Twain, *The Adventures of Huckleberry Finn*
The Homeric *Hymn to Hermes*
Karl Kerényi, *Hermes: Guide of Souls*
Richard Headstrom, *Whose Track is It? A Field Guide to Animal Tracks*
"Coyote." *The Encyclopedia Britannica,* 11th edition
William Blake, "Annotations to Bacon's *Essays Moral, Economical and Political*" and "The Mental Traveller"
White Heat, a film by Raoul Walsh